MOOLAH MATTER$

MONEY SMART

FINANCIAL JOURNAL

SONIA DIAZ

ISBN: 978-1-7332907-9-1

This book
belongs to:

____

____

____

Keeping a daily gratitude and financial journal is an excellent practice for fostering positivity and managing your finances effectively. In your journal, you can write down things you're grateful for each day, as well as track your expenses, income, savings goals, and any financial reflections or insights you have. This habit can help you stay mindful of your blessings, maintain financial discipline, and work towards your financial objectives.

MOOLAH
MATTER$

SETTING SMART GOALS

Goal 1:

Specific — What do I want to accomplish and why?

Measurable — How will I know when I have accomplished it?

Achievable — How can I accomplish this goal?

Relevant — Is this the right time for me to be working toward this goal?

Timebound — When do I want to accomplish this goal by?

Goal 2:

Specific.

Measurable.

Achievable.

Relevant.

Timebound.

Goal 3:

Specific.

Measurable.

Achievable.

Relevant.

Timebound.

Goal 4:

Specific.

Measurable.

Achievable.

Relevant.

Timebound.

JANUARY

Goal

Action Plan | **Date**

.... | ....

.... | ....

.... | ....

.... | ....

.... | ....

Grateful For

....

....

....

....

....

To Improve

....

....

....

....

....

Notes

....

....

....

....

JANUARY
Monthly Budget

Income	
Income 1	
Income 2	
Other Income	
Total	

Expenses
Month
Budget

To be paid	Due Date	Amount	Paid	Notes

Summary

Total Income	Total Expenses	Difference

Notes

JANUARY--FRESH START

"A budget is more than numbers--it's your vision for the future written in dollars and cents." ~ Moolah Matter$

Affirmation: This month, I choose progress over perfection.

Financial Goal:

GRATITUDE JOURNAL

GRATITUDE JOURNAL

GRATITUDE JOURNAL

FEBRUARY

Goal

Action Plan

Date

Grateful For

To Improve

Notes

FEBRUARY

Monthly Budget

Income	
Income 1	
Income 2	
Other Income	
Total	

Expenses
Month
Budget

To be paid	Due Date	Amount	Paid	Notes

Summary		
Total Income	Total Expenses	Difference

Notes

FEBRUARY-- SELF-WORTH & WEALTH

"Know your worth, then add tax. Your finances should reflect your confidence." ~ Moolah Matter$

Affirmation: I am worthy of wealth and prepared to manage it wisely.

Financial Goal:

GRATITUDE JOURNAL

GRATITUDE JOURNAL

GRATITUDE JOURNAL

MARCH

Goal

Action Plan

Date

Grateful For

To Improve

Notes

MARCH
Monthly Budget

Income	
Income 1	
Income 2	
Other Income	
Total	

Expenses
Month
Budget

To be paid	Due Date	Amount	Paid	Notes

Summary

Total Income	Total Expenses	Difference

Notes

MARCH--GROWTH MINDSET

"Money grows where discipline is planted. Water your goals with consistency." ~ Moolah Matter$

Affirmation: I commit to consistency, not comparison.

Financial Goal:

GRATITUDE JOURNAL

GRATITUDE JOURNAL

GRATITUDE JOURNAL

APRIL

Goal

Action Plan **Date**

....

....

....

....

....

Grateful For

....

....

....

....

....

To Improve

....

....

....

....

....

Notes

....

....

....

....

APRIL
Monthly Budget

Income	
Income 1	
Income 2	
Other Income	
Total	

Expenses
Month
Budget

To be paid	Due Date	Amount	Paid	Notes

Summary

Total Income	Total Expenses	Difference

Notes

APRIL--FINANCIAL LITERACY MONTH

"Financial education isn't a luxury—it's the foundation for freedom." ~ Moolah Matter$

Affirmation: I am a lifelong learner on the road to financial freedom.

Financial Goal:

GRATITUDE JOURNAL

GRATITUDE JOURNAL

GRATITUDE JOURNAL

MAY

Goal

Action Plan

Date

Grateful For

To Improve

Notes

MAY
Monthly Budget

Income	
Income 1	
Income 2	
Other Income	
Total	

Expenses
Month
Budget

To be paid	Due Date	Amount	Paid	Notes

Summary		
Total Income	Total Expenses	Difference

Notes

MAY--PURPOSE & PROSPERITY

"Don't just chase money. Build a life so valuable that money follows your purpose." ~ Moolah Matter$

Affirmation: My purpose attracts prosperity.

Financial Goal:

GRATITUDE JOURNAL

GRATITUDE JOURNAL

GRATITUDE JOURNAL

JUNE

Goal

Action Plan | **Date**

....

....

....

....

....

Grateful For

....

....

....

....

....

To Improve

....

....

....

....

....

Notes

....

....

....

....

JUNE

Monthly Budget

Income	
Income 1	
Income 2	
Other Income	
Total	

Expenses
Month
Budget

To be paid	Due Date	Amount	Paid	Notes

Summary		
Total Income	Total Expenses	Difference

Notes

JUNE-- MID-YEAR CHECK-IN

"Review. Reset. Refocus. Progress is made by those who pause to plan." ~ Moolah Matter$

Affirmation: Reflection strengthens my results.

Financial Goal:

GRATITUDE JOURNAL

GRATITUDE JOURNAL

GRATITUDE JOURNAL

JULY

Goal

Action Plan | **Date**

Grateful For

To Improve

Notes

JULY

Monthly Budget

Income	
Income 1	
Income 2	
Other Income	
Total	

Expenses
Month
Budget

To be paid	Due Date	Amount	Paid	Notes

Summary

Total Income	Total Expenses	Difference

Notes

JULY--FREEDOM & INDEPENDENCE

"True independence isn't about having it all—it's about owning your choices." ~ Moolah Matter$

Affirmation: I take ownership of my financial destiny.

Financial Goal:

GRATITUDE JOURNAL

GRATITUDE JOURNAL

GRATITUDE JOURNAL

AUGUST

Goal

Action Plan | **Date**

Grateful For

To Improve

Notes

AUGUST

Monthly Budget

Income	
Income 1	
Income 2	
Other Income	
Total	

Expenses
Month
Budget

To be paid	Due Date	Amount	Paid	Notes

Summary

Total Income	Total Expenses	Difference

Notes

AUGUST-- WEALTH BUILDING

"Wealth isn't built overnight—it's built daily through smart decisions and small wins." ~ Moolah Matter$

Affirmation: Small wins create lasting wealth.

Financial Goal:

GRATITUDE JOURNAL

GRATITUDE JOURNAL

GRATITUDE JOURNAL

SEPTEMBER

Goal

Action Plan | **Date**

Grateful For

To Improve

Notes

SEPTEMBER

Monthly Budget

Income	
Income 1	
Income 2	
Other Income	
Total	

Expenses
Month
Budget

To be paid	Due Date	Amount	Paid	Notes

Summary		
Total Income	Total Expenses	Difference

Notes

SEPTEMBER--LEGACY MONTH

"Don't just make a living—make a legacy. What you teach about money lasts for generations." ~ Moolah Matter$

Affirmation: My financial habits will outlive me.

Financial Goal:

GRATITUDE JOURNAL

GRATITUDE JOURNAL

GRATITUDE JOURNAL

OCTOBER

Goal

Action Plan | **Date**

....

....

....

....

....

Grateful For

....

....

....

....

....

To Improve

....

....

....

....

....

Notes

....

....

....

....

OCTOBER
Monthly Budget

Income	
Income 1	
Income 2	
Other Income	
Total	

Expenses
Month
Budget

To be paid	Due Date	Amount	Paid	Notes

Summary

Total Income	Total Expenses	Difference

Notes

OCTOBER--CONFIDENCE & COURAGE

"Fear fades when knowledge grows. Learn the rules of money, then rewrite them your way." ~ Moolah Matter$

Affirmation: I am a lifelong learner on the road to financial freedom.

Financial Goal:

GRATITUDE JOURNAL

GRATITUDE JOURNAL

GRATITUDE JOURNAL

NOVEMBER

Goal

Action Plan

Date

Grateful For

To Improve

Notes

NOVEMBER

Monthly Budget

Income	
Income 1	
Income 2	
Other Income	
Total	

Expenses
Month
Budget

To be paid	Due Date	Amount	Paid	Notes

Summary		
Total Income	Total Expenses	Difference

Notes

NOVEMBER--GRATITUDE & GROWTH

"Gratitude turns earnings into abundance. The more thankful you are, the richer you feel." ~ Moolah Matter$

Affirmation: I appreciate what I have and attract more.

Financial Goal:

GRATITUDE JOURNAL

GRATITUDE JOURNAL

GRATITUDE JOURNAL

DECEMBER

Goal

Action Plan | **Date**

.... | ....
.... | ....
.... | ....
.... | ....
.... | ....

Grateful For

....
....
....
....
....

To Improve

....
....
....
....
....

Notes

....
....
....
....

DECEMBER

Monthly Budget

Income	
Income 1	
Income 2	
Other Income	
Total	

Expenses
Month
Budget

To be paid	Due Date	Amount	Paid	Notes

Summary

Total Income	Total Expenses	Difference

Notes

DECEMBER--REFLECTION & RENEWAL

"Close the year strong. Count lessons, not losses—and start the next chapter wiser." ~ Moolah Matter$

Affirmation: I am a lifelong learner on the road to financial freedom.

Financial Goal:

GRATITUDE JOURNAL

GRATITUDE JOURNAL

GRATITUDE JOURNAL

MEETING AGENDA

DATE

LOCATION

PROJECTS

-
-
-

DISCUSSION

ATTENDEES

NOTES

-
-
-
-
-
-
-
-
-
-
-
-
-

PRIORITY

NOTES

MEETING AGENDA

DATE

LOCATION

PROJECTS

-
-
-

DISCUSSION

ATTENDEES

NOTES

-
-
-
-
-
-
-
-
-
-
-
-
-

PRIORITY

NOTES

MEETING AGENDA

DATE

LOCATION

PROJECTS

-
-
-

DISCUSSION

ATTENDEES

NOTES

-
-
-
-
-
-
-
-
-
-
-
-
-

PRIORITY

NOTES

MEETING AGENDA

DATE

LOCATION

PROJECTS

-
-
-

DISCUSSION

ATTENDEES

NOTES

-
-
-
-
-
-
-
-
-
-
-
-
-

PRIORITY

NOTES

MEETING AGENDA

DATE

LOCATION

PROJECTS

-
-
-

DISCUSSION

ATTENDEES

NOTES

-
-
-
-
-
-
-
-
-
-
-
-
-

PRIORITY

NOTES

MEETING AGENDA

DATE

LOCATION

PROJECTS

- ....
- ....
- ....

DISCUSSION

ATTENDEES

NOTES

- ....
- ....
- ....
- ....
- ....
- ....
- ....
- ....
- ....
- ....
- ....
- ....
- ....

PRIORITY

NOTES

MEETING AGENDA

DATE

LOCATION

PROJECTS

-
-
-

DISCUSSION

ATTENDEES

NOTES

-
-
-
-
-
-
-
-
-
-
-
-
-

PRIORITY

NOTES

MEETING AGENDA

DATE

LOCATION

PROJECTS

- ....
- ....
- ....

DISCUSSION

ATTENDEES

NOTES

- ....
- ....
- ....
- ....
- ....
- ....
- ....
- ....
- ....
- ....
- ....
- ....
- ....

PRIORITY

NOTES

MEETING AGENDA

DATE

LOCATION

PROJECTS

-
-
-

DISCUSSION

ATTENDEES

NOTES

-
-
-
-
-
-
-
-
-
-
-
-
-

PRIORITY

NOTES

MEETING AGENDA

DATE

LOCATION

PROJECTS

-
-
-

DISCUSSION

ATTENDEES

NOTES

-
-
-
-
-
-
-
-
-
-
-
-
-

PRIORITY

NOTES

MEETING AGENDA

DATE

LOCATION

PROJECTS

-
-
-

DISCUSSION

ATTENDEES

NOTES

-
-
-
-
-
-
-
-
-
-
-
-
-

PRIORITY

NOTES

MEETING AGENDA

DATE

LOCATION

PROJECTS

- ....
- ....
- ....

DISCUSSION

ATTENDEES

NOTES

- ....
- ....
- ....
- ....
- ....
- ....
- ....
- ....
- ....
- ....
- ....
- ....
- ....

PRIORITY

NOTES

MEETING AGENDA

DATE

LOCATION

PROJECTS

-
-
-

DISCUSSION

ATTENDEES

NOTES

-
-
-
-
-
-
-
-
-
-
-
-
-

PRIORITY

NOTES

MEETING AGENDA

DATE

LOCATION

PROJECTS

-
-
-

DISCUSSION

ATTENDEES

NOTES

-
-
-
-
-
-
-
-
-
-
-
-
-

PRIORITY

NOTES

MOOLAH
MATTER$

Made in the USA
Monee, IL
02 November 2026

67383863R00059